Foreword

This cookbook started life as a challenge I made to my mom in 2006! I asked her to document her favorite dishes so that future generations would be able to enjoy her dishes in all their glory. Since then, many a night, my mom could be found in front of our home computer, typing slowly on the keyboard. My mom lost several iterations of the recipes due to various inconceivable hard drive crashes and word processor issues. Despite these "technical difficulties," my mom was even more determined to write down her recipes. After every setback, she rededicated herself to the project with even more vigor and determination!

Well, you may ask who this wizard of Kerala cuisine is! Chandrika Pathiyal was born in 1942 in the village of Kurumassery in Kerala, India. After marrying my father, Vasudevan Pathiyal, she dutifully headed to the local Home Science College in Angamaly, Kerala, to further hone her cooking skills. There, she expanded her knowledge of dishes from every corner of Kerala, typically not found in her small village. In 1973, she migrated to Canada with two young sons to join my father. Over the years, she built up a reputation among her family and friends for being exceptionally talented in preparing tasty Kerala cuisine - including my perennial favorite snacks: pappada vada and tuna cutlets.

I am confident you will enjoy the recipes herein, just as I did all my life, prepared by my loving mom, and now published to celebrate her 80th birthday!

Enjoy!

Krishna K. Pathiyal

This book is dedicated to my grandchildren, Milind, Hrishi, Leela, Dhillon and Nikki. I hope they make a few of these dishes for themselves and their children one day!

Chandrika Pathiyal

SNACKS

01

POTATO BONDA

A hot spicy snack best served with tea on a rainy evening! Bonda translates to a ball shaped fritter. This dish is a common South Indian street food snack.

PREP : 10 mins   COOK : 30 mins   SERV : 8

INGREDIENTS

Potatoes	3 medium
Green chillies	4
Onion	1 big
Ginger	1-inch piece
Curry leaves	A few
Mustard seeds	1 tbs
Besan flour	1 cup
Asafetida	1/4 tsp
Chilly powder	1 tsp
Turmeric powder	1/2 tsp
Oil	1 cup
Baking powder	1/2 tsp
Water	Enough to make batter

METHOD

- Wash and cook the potatoes. In a big bowl, take besan flour, baking powder, chilly powder, 1/4 teaspoon turmeric powder, asafetida, and salt. Mix well and add water to make the batter. The batter should have the consistency of pancake batter. Cover the batter and keep it aside.

- Cut the onion into long slices. Chop ginger and green chillies. Skin the cooked potato and mash it a little bit such that there are a few small pieces too.

- Heat 2 teaspoons of oil in a pan and add mustard seeds. When the mustard seeds splutter, add chillies, ginger, and curry leaves. Mix well and add the sliced onion. When onion turns brown, add 1/4 teaspoon turmeric powder, mashed potatoes, and salt. Add a little water and mix well for a few seconds.

- Remove from heat and set aside to cool. Once the mixture cools, shape it into small lime-sized balls.

- Heat oil in a pan. Dip the potato balls into the batter. Ensure all sides are covered in batter. Fry four balls at a time in the oil. Once they are lightly brown, remove from oil with a slotted spoon and place them on paper towels. Serve them hot with ketchup or mint chutney.

ETHAKKA APPAM (BANANA FRITTERS)

Easy to make, banana fritters or sweet banana bajjis are an ideal tea time snack.

PREP : 5 mins   COOK : 15 mins   SERV : 6

INGREDIENTS

Ripe plantain banana	3
Besan or rice flour	1-1/2 cups
Baking powder	1 tsp
Turmeric powder	1/2 tsp
Water	Enough to make a thin batter
Salt	To taste
Oil	2 cups

METHOD

- Wash and peel the plantain banana. Cut into half, then cut each half lengthwise into 3 long slices. Mix the flour with water, turmeric powder, and salt to make a batter (that is of a pancake batter consistency).

- Heat oil in a frying pan. Dip the sliced banana pieces in batter, ensuring all sides are covered well. Then drop the banana slices in the oil (no more than three slices at a time). After 2 minutes, turn the slices over. Do not let either side get burned. After the second side is cooked, take the banana pieces out of the oil with a big slotted spoon, allowing the oil to drain back into the pan, and then place on a paper towel.

- Add more paper towels to absorb excess oil from the fried banana slices. If the banana is not sweet enough, you may add some sugar into the batter.

IDLI UPPUMAVU

A very simple but delicious teatime snack, this salt variation of unniappam can be made when you have left over idli batter. This is an excellent recipe to try when you have unexpected guests.

PREP : 10 mins (if you have idli batter available)   COOK : 20 mins   SERV : 10

INGREDIENTS

Ingredient	Quantity
Idli batter	2 cups
Green chillies	4
Red small onion	6
Ginger	1-inch piece
Sooji (rava)	2 tbs
Curry leaves	A little
Oil	1/4 cup
Water	Sufficient quantity
Salt	to Taste

METHOD

- Mix sooji (rava) with 1-1/2 tablespoons water. Add the idli batter. Add chopped green chillies, ginger, onion and curry leaves, and combine them into the batter.

- Heat the appakara and pour 1 teaspoon of oil into each holder. Then pour a spoon of batter into each holder (do not fill up the holder). Cook for a minute and then turn over. Cook for one more minute and take out the appams. The appams are ready. Arrange them on a plate and serve them hot.

UNNIAPPAM

Also called neyyappam, unniappam is a sweet that is made in a special pan for deep frying called "appakara." Appakaras come in various sizes – accommodating 4, 5, or 7 unniappams.

PREP : 15 mins to make the batter and 3 hours to let the batter rest
COOK : 40 mins   SERV : 10

INGREDIENTS

Rice flour	1-1/2 cup
Jaggery or brown sugar	1-3/4 cup
Cumin powder	2 tsp
Dry ginger powder	1 tsp
Cardamom powder	1 tsp
Water	Sufficient amount
Ghee or oil	1 cup
Coconut bits	3 cup
Ripe bananas	4

METHOD

• Fry the coconut bits in one tablespoon ghee and keep aside. Peel the bananas and mash them in a bowl with your hand. In another bowl, add flour, jaggery, cumin powder, dry ginger powder, cardamom powder, coconut bits, a little water, and mix well. Combine this with the mashed banana. The mixture should have a pancake batter consistency. Keep aside for three hours.

• Pour oil in the appam holders in the "appakara" and when it is hot, pour the batter, but do not fill more than half of the holder. Two minutes later, turn the appam over. Do not let either side get burnt. After both sides are brown, remove from the oil onto a paper towel. Add oil in the holder as required for frying the remaining appams.

Note: You can refrigerate this appam. If you do not have the "appakara," you could make the appams in a deep-frying pan by directly pouring about a ladle of batter into the oil.

JACKFRUIT ADA

Chakka Ada is a steamed jackfruit filled rice cake. It is a traditional Kerala dish that is usually made when the jackfruit is in season. If jackfruit is not available, "chakka varatti" or condensed jackfruit pulp (jackfruit jam) could be used.

PREP : 15 mins   COOK : 10 mins   SERV : 8

INGREDIENTS

Jackfruit pieces	2 cups
Jaggery	1 cup
Shredded coconut	1/2 cup
Coconut bits	2 tbs
Rice flour	2 cups
Cardamom powder	2 tsp
Salt	One pinch
Ghee	2 tbs
Aluminum foil	6-inch square sheet
Water	Sufficient quantity

METHOD

- Melt jaggery in a pan with sufficient water. When the water reduces, add shredded coconut and cardamom. Add coconut bits, mix well, and remove the pan from the stove. Add the jackfruit pieces and mash well. Now add rice flour, salt, and mix thoroughly with hand (do not use water).

- Shape the jackfruit mix into small balls, each about the size of a small lemon. Spread some ghee on an aluminum foil. Place a jackfruit ball on the sheet and press it lightly – the ada should be thick. Wrap the foil around the ada.

- Place the wrapped adas on idli cooker plates. Steam cook for 15 minutes.

- In Kerala, people use either jackfruit or banana leaves instead of aluminum foil to wrap the ada.

RICE ADA

Rice ada is a steamed rice confection with coconut and sugar/jaggery filling. This is a light snack to be consumed with afternoon chai.

PREP : 10 mins COOK : 10 mins SERV : 6

INGREDIENTS

Rice flour	3 cups
Shredded coconut	2 cups
Sugar	1/2 cup
Cardamom powder	1 tsp
Ghee	2 tbs
Salt	A pinch
Aluminum foil	5-inch square sheet
Boiled water	4 cups

METHOD

- Boil the water with salt. Mix the water to the rice flour and knead the flour to make nice, soft dough. Cut the aluminum foil into 5-inch square sheets and lightly spread ghee on each sheet. Add cardamom powder to the shredded coconut. Make lemon-sized balls from the dough. Place the balls on the aluminum sheet and press them flat with your fingers to cover the whole sheet. On one half of the flattened dough, place 3 teaspoons of shredded coconut. Sprinkle one teaspoon sugar on top of this and fold down the middle. Fold the edges a little bit. Use the rest of the dough balls to make more adas.

- Place the prepared adas in idli stand plates and steam them in an idli cooker for about 10 minutes. Take it out and serve it hot.

- Instead of sugar, you can also use jaggery. Melt jaggery with a little water in a pan. When the jaggery thickens, add the shredded coconut and cardamom. Mix well until the coconut dries up and remove pan from heat. Then follow the same method to make the ada.

FRIED CHICKEN

A very popular and tasty snack – an anytime favorite.

PREP : 35 mins including marinating   COOK : 30 mins   SERV : 4

INGREDIENTS

Medium size boneless chicken pieces	10
All purpose flour	1 cup
Eggs	2
Chilly powder	3 tsp
Garlic ginger paste	2 tbs
Green chillies	12
Tomatoes	2
Curry leaves	A few
Salt	To taste
Vinegar	1 tbs
Garam masala	1 tbs
Oil	1/2 cup

METHOD

- Wash the chicken pieces well. Beat the eggs, add chilly powder and salt, beat again, and then mix with flour. Add the chicken into the egg-flour mixture and leave aside for 30 minutes.

- Cut the tomatoes and green chillies lengthwise.

- Heat oil in a frying pan and fry the chicken pieces in low heat. Take it out and keep it aside.

- In the same pan in about 2 tablespoons oil), add the green chillies, ginger-garlic paste and garam masala, and stir until the green chillies become tender. Then add tomatoes, vinegar, and salt. Stir for a few seconds. Add the fried chicken pieces into the masala. Cover and cook on low heat for 10 minutes. Serve hot.

CASSAVA BOILED WITH CHILLY CHUTNEY

Cassava is an inherent part of Kerala cuisine. It is rich in carbohydrates and is craved for the texture it gives to a dish. The easiest way to have cassava is by boiling it and having it with chilly chutney.

PREP : 5 mins   COOK : 10 mins   SERV : 4

INGREDIENTS

Frozen cassava	1/2 kg
Water	5 cups
Chilly powder	1 tbs
Red (small) onions	5
Salt	To taste
Curry leaves	A few
Oil	1 tbs

METHOD

- Cut the cassava into 2-inch pieces. Boil the cassava pieces in 5 cups of water in a pot and cook for 10 minutes. When cassava is almost cooked, add salt. Do not overcook. Some cassava varieties cook very quickly.

- Drain the water out and place the cassava pieces in a bowl.

- For chilly chutney: Grind chilly powder, onion, salt, and curry leaves together for 3 to 5 seconds. Pour the chutney in a small bowl and add oil.

- Serve the cassava with the chilly chutney.

TUNA CUTLET

Tuna cutlets serve as a good appetizer. You can also serve them as snacks during tea time or have them as side dish for dinner. All the young people seem to really enjoy this snack – perhaps it is the new twist to using tuna that is compelling!

🍢 PREP : 10 mins   🍲 COOK : 1 hour   📷 SERV : 10

INGREDIENTS

Tuna cans (small)	2
Potatoes (big)	2
Onions (big)	2
Green chillies	8
Ginger	1-inch piece
Garlic	2 tsp, chopped
Cinnamon	1 tsp
Eggs	2
Bread crumbs	3 cups
Oil	3 cups

METHOD

- Place tuna in a pan with a dollop of oil.Cover and cook for 15 to 25 minutes on low heat. Drain the stock from the meat. Mash the meat well. In the meantime, boil the potatoes, peel and then mash them very well.

- Break the eggs, separate the yolk carefully. Put the egg whites into a bowl. For this recipe, use only the whites.

- Mix the meat and potatoes.

- Cut the onions, green chillies, garlic, and ginger into small pieces. Fry them in a pan together with a tablespoon of oil for a few seconds. When the onions turn brown, add cloves, cinnamon, and salt.Add the tuna mixture and mix well.

- In a deep-frying pan, heat oil. Divide the meat into small lime-sized balls. Flatten them into oval shapes, dip them in the well-beaten egg white, and roll them in the breadcrumbs. Deep fry about 4 cutlets at a time. When both sides are brown, take them out from the oil and place them on paper towels to drain the excess oil.

Note: Make sure the oil is hot enough before frying, or else the cutlet will break.

VEGETABLE CUTLET

Tasty and nutritious, vegetable cutlets can be served at any time – as appetizers, as a teatime snack, or as a dinner side dish.

PREP : 30 mins   COOK : 1 hour   SERV : 10

INGREDIENTS

Carrots	2, grated
Cooked peas	2 cups
Potato (big)	3
Onion	1 cup, chopped
Cabbage	2 cup, finely chopped
Chilly powder	2 tsp
Turmeric powder	1/2 tsp
Cumin powder	1 tsp
Green chillies	8, chopped
Garlic	4 cloves, chopped
Salt	To taste
Bread crumbs	3 cups
Oil	3 cups
Eggs	3

METHOD

- Wash and cook the potatoes; then peel and mash them well. Heat 2 tablespoons oil in a pan. Add the chopped onions and garlic and stir. When the onions turn a light brown color, add the cooked peas, grated carrots and the finely chopped cabbage. Add salt, chilly, turmeric and cumin. Stir well.

- Cover and cook on low flame for 5 minutes without adding water. Remove the pan from heat. After the vegetables cool, add the mashed potatoes. If required, add a little more salt. Mix well. Shape the mix into oval cutlets.

- Use a deep bowl to beat the eggs well. Heat oil in a deep pan. Dip the cutlet in the eggs, roll them in bread crumbs, and fry on medium heat. Serve hot.

Note: For those pure vegetarians, instead of eggs, a batter made of white flour can also be used.

COCONUT CHUTNEY

Coconut chutney is the preferred side dish for many South Indian dishes. There are many ways to prepare coconut chutney. Here is a recipe for a spicy Kerala-style chutney.

PREP : 5 mins   COOK : 2 mins   SERV : 6

INGREDIENTS

Shredded coconut	1/2 cup
Green chillies	4
Ginger	1 inch cube
Small red onions	A few
Curry leaves	A few
Oil	1 tbs
Mustard seeds	1 tsp
Dry red chillies	2 (split into two pieces)
Salt	To taste

METHOD

- Wash the green chillies, onions, and ginger. Peel the onions and ginger. Roughly grind the shredded coconut, green chillies, ginger, onion, and curry leaves with a little water. Pour the mix into a bowl. Add salt and 1 cup water and mix well. Heat one tablespoon oil in a pan and then add mustard seeds. When the mustard splutters, add red chilly pieces and curry leaves. Now pour the chutney mix into the frying pan and stir. After a few seconds, remove the pan from the stove. Do not let the chutney boil.

Note: Idli, dosa, and urad dal vada taste best with coconut chutney.

IDLI PODI

Idli podi is a good substitute for coconut chutney. Mix 1-2 teaspoons of idli podi with sufficient oil (mustard/coconut) and use it as a side dish for idli or dosa. Idli podi is prepared well in advance and used when needed. It can be stored for a long time when kept in an airtight container.

✎ PREP : 1 minute 🝰 COOK : 10 mins 🍲 SERV : 20

INGREDIENTS

Urad dal	**2 cups**
Dry red chillies	**15**
Asafetida	**1 tsp**
Salt	**Sufficient quantity**

METHOD

- Dry roast urad dal in a hot frying pan, stirring constantly until the dal changes color and gives out an aroma. Transfer the dal onto a paper and allow it to cool. Fry the red chillies in the same pan in medium heat for 30 seconds and keep it aside in a plate.

- Heat asafetida and salt for 2 seconds in the pan and remove.

- Grind chillies and dal. Then add asafetida and salt and blend them for a minute. Allow the mix to cool and then store it in an airtight container.

MODHAKAM

Modhakams are sweet rice dumplings prepared from rice flour and jaggery and shredded coconut mixture. Though this dish is typically associated with Ganesh Chathurthi, it can also be made as a breakfast item or as a 4 o'clock snack.

PREP : 10 mins   COOK : 15 mins   SERV : 10

INGREDIENTS

Rice flour	2 cups
Salt	To taste
Shredded coconut	2 cups
Jaggery	1-1/2 cups
Water	1 Cup
Dry ginger powder	1 tsp
Cardamom powder	1 tsp

METHOD

- Mix the flour with salt. Add boiled water into the flour and mix well to make dough.

- Heat 1 cup of water in a pan, add the jaggery and keep stirring until it melts. Remove from flame and drain the jaggery (to separate any impurities). Heat the jaggery again in a pan and keep stirring until it thickens. Add shredded coconut, dry ginger powder, cardamom powder and mix well. Remove from the flame.

- Make lemon-size balls from the dough. Flatten them, place some coconut-jaggery mixture in the middle, and reshape the dough again into a ball.

- Steam cook in an idli cooker for about 15 minutes.

CURD VADA (DAHI VADA)

Curd vada is a chaat item prepared by soaking vadas in thick yogurt. This snack is ideal for parties in the summer time.

🍳 PREP : 2-1/2 hours   🍚 COOK : 30 mins   🍱 SERV : 12

INGREDIENTS

Ingredient	Amount
Urad dal (split black lentils)	1 cup
Green chillies	8
Ginger	1-Inch piece
Curry leaves	A few
Salt	To taste
Curd	2 cups
Oil	2 cups
Coriander leaves	A bunch
Water	1 cup

METHOD

• Soak the dal in 2 cups of water for two hours. Chop the green chillies and ginger into small pieces. Drain the dal and grind. Finally, add green chillies, ginger, salt and curry leaves, and grind for two minutes. Use the food processor for grinding because you can grind without water. Use a little water if needed. If more water is used, it will be difficult to shape the batter into vadas.

• Pour the batter into a large bowl. Heat oil in a deep pan. In a small bowl, pour 1 cup of water and keep it handy. When the oil is hot enough, wet your hand in the bowl and take a small quantity of batter and place it in your left hand. Press softly and make a hole in the middle of the batter with your finger. Slide the shaped batter gently into the oil. Ideally, you could put four or five vadas at a time. After a minute, turn it over. When both sides are lightly brown, remove the vada from the oil and it place on a paper towel. Right away, put the vada in cold water and squeeze it so that all the oil comes out and then put it in a bowl. Make the remaining vadas in the same manner.

• Take a shallow rectangular serving dish. Add 3 cups plain yogurt and some salt. When vadas have cooled down, place them in the dish so that they are completely covered by the yogurt. To garnish, sprinkle some coriander leaves on top of the yogurt. Keep the dahi vadas in the fridge for at least three hours.

• We can make urad dal vada (uzhunnu vada) in the same way. When vada is fried, take it out from the oil and put it on a paper towel. Do not put in water or squeeze. You can eat "uzhunnu vada" right away with sambar or coconut chutney. Or else, you could just eat it with tea.

PAPPADA VADA

A favorite teatime snack in Kerala – crispy, crunchy pappada vada is very easy to make and very tasty.

PREP : 5 mins   COOK : 15 mins   SERV : 8

INGREDIENTS

Plain pappad	8
Rice flour	1/4 cup
Salt	A pinch
Chilly powder	1/2 tsp
Turmeric powder	1/4 tsp
Sesame seeds	1 tbs
Asafetida	1/4 tsp
Cumin seeds	1/2 tsp
Oil	1 cup

METHOD

- Mix flour with water to make a slightly thick batter that has the consistency of a pancake mixture. Then add chilly powder, turmeric powder, sesame seeds, cumin seeds, salt and asafetida. Mix well. Heat oil in a deep pan. Dip pappad into the batter, ensuring all sides are covered in the batter. Then immerse two pappads in the heated oil. After two minutes, turn them over to the other side. When the pappads turn brown and crisp, remove them from the oil and place them on a paper towel. Deep fry the remaining pappads in the same manner. Add more paper towels to absorb the excess oil from the fried pappada vada.

RASA VADA

Crispy fried vada in tangy, spicy rasam. Rasam is a semi-clear soup.

🍳 PREP : 2 hours   🍲 COOK : 30 mins   🍽 SERV : 6

INGREDIENTS

Yellow split peas (Matar dal)	1 cup
Dry red chillies	4
Onion	1
Green chillies	4
Ginger	1-inch piece
Curry leaves	A few
Oil	2 cups
Salt	To taste

METHOD

• Soak the dal and dry red chillies together in a vessel for two hours.

• Dice the green chillies, onion, and ginger, and put them in a bowl. Drain water from the dal thoroughly. First grind the red chillies, followed by the dal. Do not use water for grinding. Use the food processor to roughly grind the dal. Add diced green chillies, ginger, onion, salt, and curry leaves. Grind them all for a couple of seconds. Take out the mixture and again mix them well with your hand. Shape the mixture into lime-size balls.

• Heat oil in a pan. Take a ball, place it in your left hand, and flatten into a round shape with your right hand. Press slightly at the edges. Put the vada into the hot oil. Fry about 6 vadas at a time over medium heat. After 1 or 2 minutes, the vada turns a brown color. Turn the vada onto the other side using a slotted spoon. Do not let either side get burnt. After both sides are cooked and the vada looks crispy from the outside, remove vada from the oil with the slotted spoon onto a paper towel to remove excess oil from the fried vadas.

• Rasam recipe: Refer to recipe in this book.

• Rasa Vada: Take a deep dish to keep the vadas. When vada cool down, pour sufficient rasam to immerse the vada. Cover and refrigerate it the night before. The next day, take two vadas with rasam in a bowl and serve.

Note: Rasa vada can also be served immediately after soaking the vada in hot rasam for a few minutes.

GREEN CHILLY PACHADI

A very spicy side dish and very tasty too – try this only if you are used to spicy dishes!

PREP : 5 mins   COOK : 20 mins   SERV : 5

INGREDIENTS

Green chillies	15
Tamarind	2 tbs
Shredded coconut	1 cup
Mustard seeds	1 tsp
Asafetida	1/2 tsp
Dry red chillies	2
Salt	To taste
Curry leaves	A few
Brown sugar	3 tbs
Mustard seeds	1 tbs
Water	3 cups
Oil	1-1/2 tbs

METHOD

• Grind the coconut with one teaspoon liquid mustard and keep it aside. Wash the green chillies.

• Heat 1 tablespoon oil in a frying pan and add mustard seeds. When they splutter, add green chillies (whole), dry red chillies, curry leaves, salt, brown sugar, asafetida, and 3 cups of tamarind water. Boil and cook. When the water is reduced to about 1 cup, add turmeric powder and coconut mixture. Add 1/2 tablespoon oil. Do not boil but remove immediately from the fire.

PAKKAVADA

A crisp and spicy tea time snack, pakkavada is made with a special mold called "seva nazhi" and pakkavada "chillu."

PREP : 15 mins plus 1 hour to set the dough   COOK : 40 mins   SERV : 20

INGREDIENTS

Roasted rice flour	1 kg
Besan flour	1 kg
Dry red chillies	30
Whole black pepper	40
Asafetida	1/2 tsp
Salt	1 tbs
Ghee	2 tsp
Oil	6 cups

METHOD

- Grind together red chillies, black pepper, asafetida and salt with 1/2 cup of water. Mix rice flour, besan flour and ghee into the ground mixture and knead very well. The dough should be just like chapati dough. Cover and keep aside for 1 hour.

- Heat oil in a frying pan. Take a big lime-sized ball from the dough. Fill the mold with the ball, close it, and hold it over the oil. Now turn (or press) the seva nazhi, letting the dough fall into the oil, until enough pakkavada covers the surface of the oil.

- Remove the pakkavada from oil when it is brown and crisp. Place it on paper towel to absorb excess oil.

- Note: Pakkavada can be kept for up to 2 months. It is a good accompaniment to tea.

PALAHARAM

02

VELLAYAPPAM

Vellayappam is a traditional Kerala pancake made with rice and coconut. This appam is made in a special curved pan called "appa chatty" (available in Kerala stores), which gives the appam a lacy border. You can also make the appam in regular dosa pan.

🥄 PREP : oaking rice 3 hours, grinding 10 minutes, and raising the batter 6 hours
🍲 COOK : 2 minutes for one appam 🍽 SERV : 10

INGREDIENTS

White long grain rice	White long grain rice
Yeast	2 tsp
Sugar	3 tsp
Warm water	1/4 cup
Cooked rice	3/4 cup
Shredded coconut	2 cups
Sugar	1/2 cup
Coconut milk	1/2 cup
Egg	1
Oil	2 tbs
Salt	A pinch

METHOD

- Take rice, all the three dals, and black pepper together in a vessel. Wash very well and soak in clean water for 2 hours. Chop onion and green chillies. Drain the water and grind. Do not grind too smooth. Finally, add salt, green chillies, onion, and curry leaves. Grind for one minute and take it out. Add asafetida and mix well. The batter must be a little bit thicker than dosa batter.

- Heat the dosa pan and evenly spread 1 scoop of batter on the pan. A few seconds later, sprinkle oil on the uthappam and around it and then turn it over. When it is cooked, transfer it to a plate. You can serve this with chilly sauce.

- You can make uthappam right away after grinding. After use, store the rest of the batter in the refrigerator.

- Note: If you do not have many dals available, here is an alternative. A simpler way to make uthappam is to use 3 cups of rice and 1/4 of urad dal and 1 tablespoon of black pepper, 4 green chillies, 5 small onions and some curry leaves.

UTHAPPAM

Uthappam is a spicy thick dosa topped with onions – very delicious and easy to make.

PREP : 2-1/2 hours including soaking time of 2 hours   COOK : 5 mins   SERV : 6

INGREDIENTS

Patna Rice (long grain)	3 cup
Urad dal	1/8 cup
Moong dal	1/4 cup
Chana dal	1/4 cup
Black pepper	2 tbs
Green chillies	15
Small red onions	8
Oil	1/4 cup
Curry leaves	A few
Salt	To taste
Asafetida	3/4 tsp

METHOD

- Take rice, all the three dals, and black pepper together in a vessel. Wash very well and soak in clean water for 2 hours. Chop onion and green chillies. Drain the water and grind. Do not grind too smooth. Finally, add salt, green chillies, onion, and curry leaves. Grind for one minute and take it out. Add asafetida and mix well. The batter must be a little bit thicker than dosa batter.

- Heat the dosa pan and evenly spread 1 scoop of batter on the pan. A few seconds later, sprinkle oil on the uthappam and around it and then turn it over. When it is cooked, transfer it to a plate. You can serve this with chilly sauce.

- You can make uthappam right away after grinding. After use, store the rest of the batter in the refrigerator.

- Note: If you do not have many dals available, here is an alternative. A simpler way to make uthappam is to use 3 cups of rice and 1/4 of urad dal and 1 tablespoon of black pepper, 4 green chillies, 5 small onions and some curry leaves.

IDLI

Idli is a famous South Indian dish and it is popular all over India. It is very easy to make and if you have the batter ready, you can get this tiffin ready in minutes.

PREP : Soaking rice and dal 4 hours, grinding 40 mins, raising the batter 6 hours.
COOK : 10 mins SERV : 20

INGREDIENTS

Idli rice	3 cups
Urad dal	1 cup
Fenugreek seeds	1 tbs

METHOD

- Wash the rice, dal and fenugreek well. Soak the rice, dal and fenugreek in separate vessels for 5 hours.

- Drain the dal and grind into a fine paste, using water while you are grinding. Once it is done, pour it out into a big pot and set aside. Drain and grind the rice and fenugreek, but not as fine as the dal. Pour it into the dal batter. Add salt, stir well, and keep it covered in a warm place.

- Keep the batter overnight or for six hours to ferment. Grease the idli thattu (holder) and fill with batter. Make sure that there is enough water in the idli cooker, place the holders in the cooker, cover and cook for 10 minutes.

- Take out the holders and allow it to cool. Take out the idli with an idli spoon or a butter knife.

- Serve the idlis hot with sambar, coconut chutney or idli podi.

MASALA DOSA

Urad dal dosa stuffed with masala filling. This is a very popular South Indian tiffin.

PREP : Soaking rice and dal 3 hours, grinding 40 minutes, and for raising 5 hours.
COOK : 20 mins   SERV : 10

INGREDIENTS

White long grain rice	2 cups	Turmeric powder	1/2 tsp
Urad dal	1/8 cup	Salt	To taste
Fenugreek seeds	1 tsp	Dry red chillies	2 (split into 2)
Potatoes	10	Mustard seeds	1tbs
Green chillies	8	Curry leaves	A few
Onions	2	Oil	3 tbs
Ginger	2 inch piece	Lemon juice	3/4 tsp

METHOD

For dosa:

- Soak fenugreek seeds with urad dal in water. Soak rice in water in another pot. After 3 hours, wash the urad dal and rice. First grind the urad dal into a smooth batter. Pour it out into a large bowl. Then finely grind rice and combine it with the urad dal batter in the bowl. Add salt and mix everything together. Cover and keep it in a warm place. After 6 hours, it will rise. Then you can make dosa out of the batter.

For masala stuffing:

- Wash the potatoes and boil them in a big pot. Slice onions into long pieces. Chop the green chillies and ginger into small pieces. When the potatoes are cooked, take them out to cool. Peel and cut the potatoes into 1/2-inch cubes.

- In a heated pan, add oil and mustard seeds. When the mustard seeds splutter, add curry leaves and onion, stir for 2 minutes, and add turmeric powder, green chillies, ginger, and salt. Continue to stir for a few seconds more and then add potatoes, salt, and 1/2 cup of water. Stir it for a few seconds and finally add lemon juice. Mix well. Remove from the stove and set aside.

To make masala dosa:

- Stir the dosa batter with a ladle. The batter should have the consistency of pancake batter. If the batter is thick, add a little water to make it thin.

- Place a dosa pan (tava) on medium heat. When the pan is hot enough, scoop 1 ladle batter and pour it into the middle of the pan. Quickly spread it into a circle and cover it with a lid. After a few seconds, remove the lid and sprinkle a few drops of oil around the dosa. When the dosa is crisp, take one big spoon of potato masala, place it on one side of the dosa, and fold the dosa. Take the dosa from the pan and place it on a plate. Serve with coconut chutney or sambar.

For plain dosa:

- Pour one scoop of batter on a hot pan and spread fast into a round shape. After a few seconds, sprinkle a few drops of oil around the dosa and when it is a little crisp, turn it over. When you make plain dosa, you do not have to cover the pan.

VEGETARIAN

03

PULISSERY

Pulissery is a Kerala dish made with sour curd (or yogurt) and shredded coconut.

PREP :3 Mins   COOK : 5 mins   SERV : 4

INGREDIENTS

Shredded coconut	1 cup
Green chillies	4
Cumin seeds	1 tsp
Turmeric powder	1 tsp
Salt	To taste
Yogurt	3 cups
Curry leaves	A few
Oil	1 tbs
Dry red chillies	2
Mustard seeds	1tsp

METHOD

- Finely grind shredded coconut, green chillies, cumin seeds, and turmeric powder and finally add a few curry leaves (to slightly mash them). Pour the coconut mixture into a bowl, add yogurt and salt, and mix well.

- Heat oil in a pan and add mustard seeds. When they splutter, add red chillies (cut into 2 pieces) and pour the coconut mixture. Warm for a few seconds but do not boil. Serve with rice.

SAMBAR

Sambar is a popular South Indian preparation and is a part of almost every meal. Each state in South India has its own variant, but basically sambar is a vegetable stew with dal and tamarind. You could make sambar with vegetables like cucumber, radish, pumpkin, okra, eggplant, and yam. When you make sambar with just small red onions, it is called onion sambar. Sambar could be served with rice or as a side dish for idli, dosa, vada etc.

PREP : 10 mins   COOK : 30 mins.   SERV : 8

INGREDIENTS

Toor dal	1 cup
Potatoes	2
Onion	1
Carrot	1
Drumsticks	2
Shredded coconut	1/2 cup
Dry red chillies	6
Coriander seeds	2 tbs
Asafetida	1 tsp
Fenugreek seeds	1/2 tsp
Turmeric powder	1 tsp
Chilly powder	1 tsp
Tamarind paste	1 tbs
Oil	1 tbs
Dry red chilly	2
Mustard seeds	1 tsp
Curry leaves	A few

METHOD

- Wash all the vegetables. Peel the potatoes and cut them into cubes. Scrape the green skin off drumsticks and cut into 2-inch-long pieces. Peel the onion and cut it into 4. Cut carrots into small rounds. Put all the cut vegetables into a bowl. Wash the dal. Boil water in a pot and add dal. Add 1/2 teaspoon turmeric powder and 1/4 teaspoon oil.

- When the dal is almost cooked, add all the vegetables with 2 cups of water, salt, 1 teaspoon chilly powder, and a few curry leaves.

- Meanwhile, heat 2 teaspoons of oil in a frying pan. Add dry red chilly, coriander seeds, 1/4 teaspoon asafetida, fenugreek seeds, shredded coconut, and curry leaves and fry for 3 minutes. Take it out, grind it to a fine paste with a little water and keep it aside.

- When vegetables are cooked, add tamarind and boil for 2 minutes. Finally pour the coconut mixture into the pot. Boil for 2 minutes and remove from fire.

- Heat 1 teaspoon oil in a pan and add mustard seeds. When the mustard seeds splutter, add red chillies (cut into 2 pieces), 1/4 teaspoon asafetida, 1/4 teaspoon fenugreek seeds, and curry leaves. Stir well and pour it into the pot. Cover and keep aside.

- Note: You could use lemon juice or tomatoes instead of tamarind. You can use readymade sambar powder from Indian stores instead of ground masala.

RASAM

Rasam is a traditional South Indian thin lentil and tamarind soup. It could be served as a soup or with rice as a main dish accompanied by fried/roasted pappad. Great to be consumed on cold or rainy days!

🥄 PREP : 3 mins   🍚 COOK : 20 mins.   🍲 SERV : 4

INGREDIENTS

Dal	1/2 cup
Tamarind	20 g
Turmeric powder	1/2 tsp
Chilly powder	1 tbs
Asafetida	1 tsp
Black pepper powder	1tsp
Garlic	6 Cloves
Salt	To taste
Tomato	1
Mustard seeds	1 tsp
Water	6 cups
Oil	1 tbs
Curry leaves	A few
Coriander leaves	A few

METHOD

- Wash the dal. In a big pot, boil 6 cups of water. Add dal and cook for 20 minutes. In the meantime, soak tamarind in two cups of water and extract the tamarind juice.

- When dal is cooked, drain the dal water into a bowl. In a big pot, add tamarind extract, turmeric powder, chilly powder, asafetida, black pepper powder and garlic, and boil together about 10 minutes. Then add chopped tomatoes, dal water, curry leaves and salt, and boil for 3 more minutes. In a heated pan, add oil. Once heated, fry mustard seeds, red chillies, a pinch of Asafetida and curry leaves.

AVIYAL

Aviyal is a traditional Kerala dish that is relished by one and all and it is prepared for all major feasts. Aviyal is prepared with as many vegetables as possible. The vegetables are uniformly cut and cooked with finely ground coconut.

PREP : 10 mins   COOK : 20 mins   SERV : 6

INGREDIENTS

Drumstick	1
Carrots	50 g
Beans	50 g
Cucumber	50 g
Chilly powder	1 tbs
Turmeric powder	1/2 tsp
Green chillies	6
Salt	To taste
Shredded coconut	1 cup
Cumin seeds	1 tsp
Coconut oil	1 tbs
Garlic	2 Cloves
Small red onions	3
Curry leaves	A few
Yogurt	1 cup

METHOD

- Wash all the vegetables. Scrape the green skin off the drumstick, cut into 3/4-inch-long pieces, and put them in a pot. Peel the carrots and cucumber, cut them also into pieces of 3/4-inch length, and put them into the pot. Add chilly powder, turmeric powder, salt, a few curry leaves, 2 green chillies, and 2 cups of water. Cover and cook.

- Roughly grind shredded coconut, green chillies, garlic, onions and cumin seeds. When the vegetables are cooked, add the coconut mixture into the pot, and boil for 1 minute. Remove from fire, add yogurt. Mix well and then add 1 tablespoon oil and curry leaves.

Note: One tablespoon tamarind extract can be used instead of yogurt. If you are using tamarind, cook the vegetables, then add tamarind juice, boil for 2 minutes, and finally add the ground coconut mixture.

LONG BEANS AND PLANTAIN MEZHUKUPURATTY

An easy to make long beans and plantain stir fry.

🥄 PREP : 10 mins   🍲 COOK : 15 mins   🍽 SERV : 4

INGREDIENTS

Long beans	2 cups when cut
Green plantains	2
Turmeric powder	1 tsp
Green chillies	5, chopped
Salt	To taste
Oil	5 tbs
Small red onions	6
Dry red chillies	4
Curry leaves	A few

METHOD

- Peel the green plantains. Cut into small square pieces. Put them in a bowl with 2 cups of cold water and 1/2 teaspoon turmeric powder. Keep for 10 minutes and then drain.

- Wash the beans and cut them into 1" long pieces. Take 2 cups of water in a pot, add the chopped plantains, 1/2 teaspoon turmeric powder, and green chillies, and boil. When the plantain is half cooked, add beans and salt. Cover and cook until the water dries up, but make sure it does not get burnt.

- Mash onions and red chillies slightly.

- Heat oil in a pan, add the onion and red chilly mix, and fry for a few seconds. When the onions turn brown, add curry leaves and stir well. Add the long beans-banana mix into the pan and keep stirring on low heat until it is slightly roasted. Remove from fire.

OLAN

Olan is a traditional Kerala dish and is an important item in big feasts such as the Onam Sadhya. Children especially love it because it is less spicy and has a sweet flavor.

PREP : 3 mins COOK : 15 mins SERV : 6

INGREDIENTS

Cucumber	100 g
Green chillies	4
String beans	50 g
Coconut milk	1 cup
Curry leaves	A few
Oil	1 tbs

METHOD

- Skin the cucumber and remove the inner soft portion with seeds. Cut 1-inch square thin slices. . Wash the string beans and cut into 1-inch length pieces. Wash the green chillies. Cut it lengthwise, but do not split.

- Take 1/2 cup of coconut milk in a bowl and add 1 cup of water. Take a pot and add the cucumber, string beans, green chillies, and a few curry leaves. Add the coconut milk and boil for 15 minutes. When the vegetables are cooked and the gravy becomes thick, add salt and mash slightly with a spoon. Add another 1/2 cup of coconut milk. Do not boil. Remove from fire. Add oil and a few more curry leaves. Serve with rice.

ONION THEEYAL

A delicious thick brown onion-based gravy that is perfect for rice.

PREP : 15 mins   COOK : 15 mins   SERV : 6

INGREDIENTS

Small red onions	Cut into long slices, 2 cups
Green chillies	4
Shredded coconut	2 cups
Curry leaves	2 tbs
Coriander powder	3 tbs
Chilly powder	1tbs
Turmeric powder	1/2 tsp
Salt	To taste
Tamarind paste	1 tbs
Dry red chillies	2
Oil	4 tbs

METHOD

- Heat 2 tablespoons oil in a pan and add mustard seeds. When the seeds splutter, add red chillies (split into 2) and a few curry leaves, and stir. Then add the sliced onions and green chillies (cut lengthwise but not separated). Fry over medium heat for 10 minutes, then lower the heat. Stir until the onions turn evenly brown.

- Meanwhile, heat the rest of the oil in another pan. Add shredded coconut and some curry leaves. Keep stirring until the coconut is roasted. Then add coriander powder, chilly powder, salt, and turmeric powder, and fry for a few seconds more. Let the mixture cool and then grind into a smooth paste. Mix tamarind with 2 tablespoons of water and pour it into the mixture. Add one cup of water also. Gravy must be a little bit thick. Once the onions are roasted, pour the coconut mixture into the pan, mix well, and boil for 4 minutes. Serve with rice.

CELERY THORAN

Celery stir fry with coconut – another traditional dish that could be made for special occasions. However, this is an essentially simple dish and could be prepared easily at any time. Celery thoran is very good with rice and chapati. Place the thoran in the chapati, roll it and eat.

PREP : 10 mins ● COOK : 5 mins ▣ SERV : 4

INGREDIENTS

Celery	1 bunch
Shredded coconut	1 cup
Green chillies	5
Garlic	4 cloves
Cumin seeds	1 tsp
Turmeric powder	1/4 tsp
Chilly powder	1/2 tsp
Chopped onion	2 tbs
Curry leaves	A few
Salt	To taste
Oil	2 tbs
Mustard seeds	2 tsp
Dry red chillies	2 (split in half)

METHOD

- Wash the celery in water. Peel off a few spines from the celery stalk. Cut it into small pieces (bite size). Lightly grind coconut, cumin seeds, green chilies, and garlic into a coarse paste. Finally add some curry leaves, grind for a few seconds, then pour it out and set aside.

- Heat oil in a frying pan and add mustard seeds. When the mustard seeds splutter, add red chillies and chopped onions. Stir until the onions turn to a golden brown color. Add curry leaves, celery, and spices. Stir, cook for 3 minutes in high heat, and then turn to medium heat. Add salt and the coconut mixture. Cover and cook for 2 minutes only. Remove from the stove.

POTATO THORAN

Potato thoran is dry dish made of finely chopped potatoes.
It is served as a side dish for rice.

PREP : 7 mins   COOK : 5 mins   SERV : 5

INGREDIENTS

Potatoes, medium size	6
Mustard seeds	1 tsp
Dry red chillies	2
Curry leaves	A few
Chana dal	1 tbs
Urad dal	3 tbs
Green chillies	4
Asafetida	1/2 tsp
Cumin seeds	1 tsp
Salt	To taste
Shredded coconut	1/2 cup
Oil	2 tbs

METHOD

- Wash the potatoes and cut them into small chunks and then wash again. Wash green chillies and cut into small pieces.

- shredded coconut, cumin seeds, green chillies, and a few curry leaves. (Mash them with your hands or use a chapati rolling pin or blender).

- Heat oil in a pan. Add mustard seeds and when they splutter, add dry red chillies (cut into 2), chana dal, urad dal, and curry leaves. Stir for 2 minutes. Add potatoes, coconut mixture, salt and asafetida. Stir and cover, cook on medium heat for only 4 minutes. Do not overcook. Remove from fire.

CHAMMANTHI

04

GINGER CHAMMANTHI

My dear mother made this chammanthi whenever one of her children complained of stomach ache or had a loss of appetite. This herbal remedy of sorts is both yummy and ready in a jiffy with just four ingredients.

PREP : 3 mins   COOK : 5 mins   SERV : 5

INGREDIENTS

Ginger	two 2"pieces
Red small onions	5
Salt	to taste
Oil	1 tsp

METHOD

- Peel ginger and onions. Grind together (but not too finely) with salt. Pour it into a bowl and add oil.

CHUTTA CHAMMANTHI

An authentic side dish from Kerala, chutta chammanthi is made from roasted coconut slices. Unlike chutney, chammanthi is of a thicker, drier paste consistency. It is very spicy and delicious. This coconut chammanthi is especially useful when someone is convalescing and does not have an appetite. As part of a simple diet, they can have a small portion of the chammanthi with rice (just do not make it too spicy).

PREP : 5 mins   COOK : 15 mins   SERV : 4

INGREDIENTS

Coconut cut into long slices	1 cup
Dry red chillies	6
Small red onions	5
Tamarind	1 tsp
Ginger	1/2 tsp, chopped
Green chilly	1
Salt	To taste
Curry leaves	A few
Oil	1 tbs
Water	Sufficient amount

METHOD

- Wash and dry the coconut slices. Heat oven to 400 degrees and roast the coconut slices on an aluminum sheet for about 7 minutes, (turning them onto the other side after 3 minutes) until they change to a dark brown color. Take the slices out, switch off the oven and place the dry chillies inside for just a few seconds.

- Wash the coconut slices. If any slices are burnt too much, remove them.

- First grind the red chillies. Then add coconut, green chillies, ginger, tamarind, salt and a bit of water to red chilli mixture. Grind to create a thick coarse paste. Finally, add onion and curry leaves and lightly grind once again. Mix together, add oil and shape the mixture into a ball. Place the chammanthi in a serving bowl.

Note: Do not use too much water when grinding.

COCONUT KATTA CHAMMANTHI

A thick coconut paste side dish that goes well with dosa, idli, and urad dal vada.

PREP : 5 mins   COOK : 3 mins   SERV : 4

INGREDIENTS

Shredded coconut	1 cup
Green chillies	4
Ginger	1-inch piece
Small red onions	5
Salt	To taste
Curry leaves	A few
Oil	1 tbs
Water	As required

METHOD

- Wash the green chillies and curry leaves. Peel and chop the ginger and onions.
- Grind the shredded coconut. Then add green chillies, ginger and salt, and grind well. Finally, add onions and curry leaves and grind only for a few seconds adding a little water.
- Add oil to the mixture. The mixture should be thick enough such that you could roll it into a ball.

CHUTTA VAZHUTHANANGA (EGGPLANT) CHAMMANTHI

This chammanthi has a unique flavor, aroma, and texture. A feast for your senses - try it and it will soon become your favorite.

PREP : 5 mins ● COOK : 20 mins SERV : 4

INGREDIENTS

Big eggplant	1
Dry red chillies	10
Tamarind paste	1 tsp
Small red onions	6
Salt	To taste
Olive oil	1 tbs
Garlic	10 cloves
Curry leaves	A few

METHOD

- Heat the oven to 400 degrees. Wash the eggplant and dry it with a paper towel. Daub olive oil over the eggplant. Peel the onions.

- Insert garlic along with the peel into the eggplant at different places and cover it with an aluminum sheet. Keep it in the oven for 15 minutes till it is roasted.

- Switch off the oven then take out the eggplant and place the dry chillies in the oven. After a few seconds, take out the chillies. Take the garlic out and peel them. In a bowl, place the eggplant and mash it with your hand. Add dry chillies, onions, garlic, tamarind, salt, and curry leaves. Mash them all together very well. Add oil.

NOTE: This goes well with rice and chapati

MANGO CHAMMANTHI

This thick paste, made of raw mangoes and coconut, is a sure fire way to spice up any boring daily fare.

🔪 PREP : 5 mins   🥘 COOK : 3 mins   🍽 SERV : 4

INGREDIENTS

Green mango, peeled and chopped	1 cup
Shredded coconut	1/2 cup
Chilly powder	2 tsp
Small red onions	3
Salt	To taste
Curry leaves	A few
Oil	1 tbs

METHOD

- Peel the onions. Grind together shredded coconut, chilly powder, mango pieces, salt, onions and curry leaves. Take it out of the blender and transfer to a bowl. Add oil and mix well.

RICE

05

LEMON RICE

An easy to make recipe, especially when you are in a hurry and you have some leftover rice.

PREP : 3 mins   COOK : 20 mins   SERV: 3

INGREDIENTS

Basmati Rice	1 cup
Ground peanuts	1/2 cup,1 tbs
Urad dal	1 tbs
Turmeric powder	1 tsp
Chilly powder	1 tsp
Asafetida	1/2 tsp
Lemon juice	2 tbs
Salt	To taste
Mustard seeds	1 tbs
Dry red chillies	6
Oil	2tbs
Curry leaves	A few
Coriander leaves	A few

METHOD

• Wash the rice. Cook the rice in 4 cups of water in a vessel for 10 minutes and drain out the water. Do not overcook.

• Spread the rice evenly on a tray to cool it.

• Heat oil in a frying pan and splutter mustard seeds. Add whole red chillies and stir well. Add ground peanuts and urad dal. Stir until the dal changes to brown color. Turn the heat low, add chilly powder, turmeric powder, asafetida, and curry leaves. Stir for a few seconds more and remove from heat.

• Mix lemon juice with salt and pour it into the rice. Add the fried masala into the rice and mix nicely.

• Garnishing suggestion: Spread lemon rice evenly on a tray. Place fried dry red chillies on the four corners and the center of the tray. Garnish with coriander leaves.

CURD RICE

A comfort dish that can be had at any time, but especially during the summer. Curd rice can also be taken to picnics.

PREP : 5 mins   COOK : 30 mins   SERV: 4

INGREDIENTS

Long grain white rice	1 cup
Yogurt	2 cups
Dry red chillies	3
Green chillies	Chopped, 2 tbs
Ginger	Chopped, 1 tbs
Salt	To taste
Milk	1/4 cup
Oil	1 tbs
Mustard seeds	2 tsp
Curry leaves	A few
Coriander leaves	A few

METHOD

- Wash the rice. Boil 4 cups of water in a pot, add rice and cook for 15 minutes. Drain and set aside to cool. Pour yogurt, milk and salt into a bowl and mix very well. Add it to the rice and mix well.

- Heat oil in a frying pan. Add mustard seeds. When it splutters, add whole red chillies. Stir until chillies turns black. Add green chillies, ginger and curry leaves. Stir it for a few seconds and then mix it well with the rice. Garnish with coriander leaves.

TOMATO RICE

Tomato rice is a popular South Indian rice dish. It is easy to make and is a great idea for a packed lunch. Also, you may enjoy it with chicken fry.

PREP : 3 mins COOK : 15 mins SERV: 3

INGREDIENTS

Patna Rice or white long grain rice	1 cup
Tomato	2 big
Chilly powder	1 tsp
Turmeric powder	1/2 tsp
Sambar powder	1 tsp
Onion	Chopped, 1 tbs
Salt	To taste
Oil	1 tbs
Mustard seeds	1 tbs
Curry leaves	A few

METHOD

- Cook the rice in 4 cups of water and drain the water. Keep it aside to cool.

- Wash the tomato and dice it. Heat oil in a frying pan, splutter mustard seeds, and add chopped onion and curry leaves. Stir until the onion turns brown. Add chilly powder, turmeric powder, and sambar powder. Stir and add the diced tomato and salt. Cook in low heat for 3 minutes. Add the rice into the tomato mix after making sure that the rice has cooled down. The tomato rice is ready.

Recipe using patna rice

Recipe using basmati rice

FISH & MEAT

06

NADAN FISH CURRY

Malayalees love seafood and many of their dishes use kudampuli (gambooge) or fish tamarind. Kudampuli is a green fruit that turns yellow when ripe. Kudampuli gets the black color after it is processed and will stay fresh for years. This nadan meen (fish) curry recipe uses kudampuli, which lends the dish a unique sour flavor. "Nadan" means country or village style preparation and basically refers to home cooking.

PREP : 10 mins   COOK : 20 mins   SERV: 5

INGREDIENTS

Sardine fish	1/2 kg
Chilly powder	2 tbs
Coriander powder	1/2 tbs
Turmeric powder	1/2 tsp
Red small onions	6
Ginger	1-inch piece
Garlic	5 cloves
Fenugreek powder	1 tsp
Gambooge (kudampuli)	2 pieces
Salt	To taste
Oil	1 tbs
Curry leaves	A few

METHOD

- Clean the fish, cut into small pieces, and put them in a pot. Peel the ginger and garlic and cut them into long slices. Soak the gambooge in 1/2 cup of water to let it dissolve partially.

- Grind chilly powder, coriander powder, turmeric powder, and onion. Add this mixture into the fish pot. Add gambooge along with the water into the pot along with ginger, garlic, curry leaves, and salt. Add another cup of water such that the fish is covered. Boil for 15 minutes. When the gravy becomes thick, add oil and fenugreek powder. Switch off the stove and leave the pot on stove.

EGG AVIYAL

Aviyal is usually made with as many vegetables as one can find. This thick gravy, however, is made using eggs cooked with chillies, onion, and coconut – a "non-veg" aviyal!

PREP : 5 mins 　 COOK : 13 mins 　 SERV: 4

INGREDIENTS

Eggs	4
Chilly powder	1-1/2 tsp
Turmeric powder	1/4 tsp
Coriander powder	1 tbs
Shredded coconut	2 cups
Cumin seeds	1/2 tsp
Red small onions	4
Salt	To taste
Curry leaves	A few
Oil	1 tbs

METHOD

- Boil water, add the eggs, and cook for just 10 minutes. Shell them and cut in half lengthwise. Grind chilly powder, turmeric powder, coriander powder, shredded coconut, cumin seeds, small onions, and curry leaves coarsely.

- Take 2 cups of water in a pot and add the mix together with green chillies, salt, eggs, and a few curry leaves. Cover and boil just for 3 minutes. Add oil and remove from heat. The gravy should be thick.

Note: Vegetarians can make the aviyal with 4 potatoes instead of eggs. Cut the peeled potatoes into long and slender pieces.

CHICKEN CURRY

Tasty chicken pieces in a spicy mint and onion gravy. Serve with rice or chapatis.

📝 PREP : 15 mins   🍲 COOK : 35 mins   🍽 SERV: 5

INGREDIENTS

Chicken thighs, medium size	1 kg
Chilly powder	2 tsp
Coriander powder	2 tbs
Turmeric powder	1/2 tsp
Garam masala powder	1/2 tsp
Cumin seeds	1 tsp
Onions	3
Tomato	1
Curry leaves	A few
Mint leaves	Chopped, 1 cup
Ginger-garlic paste	2 tbs
Salt	To taste
Oil	3 tbs

METHOD

• Wash the chicken and cut into medium pieces. Mix chilly powder, coriander powder, turmeric powder, and garam masala with a little water to make a paste and keep aside.

• Dice the tomato and onions. Grind the mint leaves. Heat oil in a pan and add mustard seeds. When the mustard seeds splutter, add cumin seeds, chopped onions, and curry leaves. Fry the onions until they turn brown and then add 2 tablespoons ginger-garlic paste. Stir for a minute and add the spices paste.

• Stir for 5 minutes in low heat until the masala is cooked. Add the diced tomato, stir for 2 minutes, then add chicken and salt, and stir it for 2 more minutes. Cover and cook for 5 minutes in medium heat. Add mint paste, stir well, pour 1 cup of boiled water, and cook for 20 minutes until the chicken is tender. When the gravy thickens remove from fire and keep aside.

KURUMASSERY SPECIAL (BONELESS CHICKEN FRY)

This delicious and easy to make dish could be served as a side dish or as a starter item at parties. My dear late mother would make this once a year (remember, this was in the 1950s) when important friends or family visit.

PREP : 50 minutes (including 30 minutes to marinade the chicken)
COOK : 30 mins 	 SERV: 4

INGREDIENTS

Boneless chicken	3/4 kg
Turmeric powder	1 tsp
Whole coriander seeds	2 tbs
Whole black pepper	3 tbs
Whole red chillies	6
Small red onions	5
Salt	To taste
Curry leaves	A few
Oil	1/8 cup

METHOD

- Wash the chicken and cut into small pieces. Grind together curry leaves with turmeric powder, coriander seeds, black pepper, red chilies, red onions and salt. Marinade the chicken in the masala for 30 minutes.

- Heat 1/8 cup of oil in a pan and add the chicken pieces. Stir it for 5 minutes. When the masala turns brown, add 3 cups of hot water. Cover and cook for 25 minutes in medium heat.

- When the gravy thickens, open the lid and keep stirring until all the gravy dries up. Pour the rest of the oil and stir. Add more oil if needed. Remove from heat.

MASALA EGG FRY

Boiled eggs covered in masala and fried to perfection – a yummy treat and easy to prepare.

PREP : 3 mins plus 10 mins to marinate the egg ● COOK : 15 mins ● SERV: 4

INGREDIENTS

Eggs	4
Chilly powder	1 tbs
Coriander powder	2 tbs
Turmeric powder	1/4 tsp
Black pepper powder	1/2 tsp
Salt	To taste
Oil	2 tbs

METHOD

- Wash and boil the eggs. Remove the shell and cut the eggs slightly lengthwise without separating them. Mix all the spices and a little salt with water to make a paste. Cover the eggs uniformly with a thin layer of this masala. Leave aside to marinate for 10 minutes.

- Heat oil in a frying pan in medium heat. Add the eggs and roll the eggs in the heated oil. Continue to shallow fry the eggs in medium heat until the masala turns uniformly dark brown on all sides. Remove the pan from the heat.

KING FISH FRY

King fish is called "neimeen" in Kerala because of its oily flesh. It is considered an expensive fish, but it has a scrumptious crispy flavor and is rich in proteins, minerals, and vitamins, especially vitamin B12. This simple but tasty dish is great for parties, especially since you can prepare the fish and do the frying well ahead of the party time.

PREP : 35 mins (Marinade fish for at least 30 mins)　COOK : 10 mins　SERV: 4

INGREDIENTS

King fish	1/2 kg
Chilly powder	1-1/2 tbs
Coriander powder	2 tsp
Turmeric powder	1/4 tsp
Black pepper powder	1/2 tsp
Lemon juice	1 tsp
Salt	To taste
Oil	1/2 cup

METHOD

- Wash the fish and cut into medium size pieces. You can use vinegar or lemon juice to clean the fish.

- Make a paste of all the six ingredients with a little water. Spread the masala over the fish pieces evenly and set aside for half an hour. The more you marinate, the tastier the fish will be.

- Heat oil in a frying pan. Add fish, cover and cook in medium heat for 2 minutes. Turn the piece over and cook for 2 more minutes.

- You may refrigerate the marinated fish and fry them the next day for better taste.

PIDI AND KOZHI

Pidi are rice dumplings served with spicy kozhi (chicken) gravy. This could be served for dinner or served as a standalone afternoon snack. Children love this dish and gobble them up!

🔪 PREP : 15 mins   🍲 COOK : 10 mins for pidi and 40 mins for chicken   🍽 SERV: 6

INGREDIENTS

Chicken thighs	1/2 kg
Ginger	1 Inch piece
Green chillies	3
Coconut bits	1/4 cup
Salt	To taste
Curry leaves	A few
Cardamom	4
Cinnamon	1 inch stick
Fennel seeds	1 tsp
Coriander seeds	2 tbs
Dry red chillies	6
Whole black pepper	10
Turmeric powder	1/4 tsp
Shredded coconut	1-1/2 cup
Small red onions	20
Roasted rice flour	3/4 cup
Cumin seeds	1/4 tsp
Garlic	6 Flakes
Oil	1/4 cup
Coconut milk	1/2 cup

METHOD

• Mix together roasted rice flour, 1/4 cup shredded coconut, 1 teaspoon cumin seed, and salt. Add boiled water into the flour to make dough. Knead well and roll small balls the size of a gooseberry. Sprinkle a little flour over each ball so that the rice balls do not stick together.

• Boil 5 cups of water and add 1 teaspoon cumin seeds, mashed garlic, and salt. Place the rice balls gently in the boiling water. Stir for 5 minutes, ensuring that the balls do not stick to each other. Finally, add 1/2 cup coconut milk and remove from fire. Now pidi is ready.

• Clean the chicken and cut it into small pieces. Add chicken, ginger, coconut bits, a few curry leaves, salt, and 2 cups of water into a pot and cook in medium heat for 25 minutes. Cut onions into round slices keep it aside to frying at the end.

• Heat 2 tablespoons oil in a pan and add cardamom, cinnamon, fennel seeds, coriander seeds, dry red chillies, whole black pepper, turmeric powder, 1 cup of the remaining shredded coconut, 1 teaspoon chopped onions, and a few curry leaves. Fry until the coconut turns brown. Remove the pan from fire and grind the mix well.

• Heat oil in a frying pan and add the sliced onions. Fry until the onions turn brown. Add the ground masala with some curry leaves and stir for 2 minutes. Pour the pan contents into the chicken pot and boil again for 3 minutes. Garnish with curry leaves.

FISH MOLEE

Fish molee is a typical Kerala preparation. The word "molee" is supposed to have originated from the Spanish word "mole," which means stew. This fish stew has a lighter flavor and is less spicy than other fish curries, mainly because coconut milk is used in preparing this dish.

PREP : 35 mins (Marinade the fish for 30 mins)   COOK : 25 mins   SERV: 4

INGREDIENTS

Big slices of King Fish	500 g
Turmeric powder	1 tsp
Salt	To taste
Ginger	1 inch piece
Garlic	3 cloves
Chilly powder	2 tsp
Tomatoes	2
Green chillies	6
Onions	2
Coconut milk	2 cans
Fenugreek powder	3/4 tsp
Black pepper powder	1tsp
Curry leaves	A few
Oil	1/2 cup

METHOD

- Clean the fish and cut into medium pieces. Mix turmeric powder and salt and make a paste with a little water. Roll the fish pieces into the paste and keep it for half an hour.

- Cut the onions into round slices. Split the green chillies without separating the pieces. Mash ginger and garlic. Cut the tomatoes into round slices.

- Heat 2 tablespoons of oil in a frying pan and fry the fish, one minute for each side. Remove the fish. Add the rest of the oil into the pan and fry the onions until they turn brown. Add mashed ginger and garlic, chilly powder, green chillies, and curry leaves and stir. Pour 1 can coconut milk mixed with 1/2 cup of water into the pan and boil for 5 minutes. Add tomatoes and cook for 10 minutes in medium heat. When the gravy becomes a little bit thick, add fish and salt, and cook for another 10 minutes in medium heat. Then add fenugreek powder, black pepper powder, curry leaves and the other can of coconut milk. Do not boil. Remove from the stove.

Note: You can use a manchatti (clay pot) to cook. This will hold the heat and will continue cooking even after it is taken off the stove

PICKLES

07

GOOSEBERRY PICKLE

Gooseberry is a rich natural source of vitamin C. It is said to be a powerful antioxidant and has antibacterial properties. Some Ayurvedic preparations use gooseberry. Here is a recipe for pickling this miracle fruit – not just healthy but delicious too!

PREP : 10 mins   COOK : 20 mins   SERV: 5

INGREDIENTS

Gooseberries	1/2 kg
Chilly powder	35 g
Mustard seeds	1 tsp
Fenugreek seeds (fried and powdered)	10 g
Oil	3 tbs
Dry red chillies	7
Asafetida	15 g
Salt	50 g
Water	50 ml

METHOD

- Wash the gooseberries and boil them in water. Drain gooseberries. Heat oil in a pan and add mustard seeds. When the mustard seeds splutter, add dry red chillies. Switch off the heat, add salt and all the other spices (fenugreek, asafetida, and chilly powder), and stir. Combine the gooseberries into the pan and mix well. Once the gooseberries have cooled down, bottle up the pickle.

LEMON PICKLE

This is a simple, tasty, and easy to make Kerala-style lemon pickle. I had the opportunity to make this pickle recently in California using lemon plucked from a backyard collection of lemon trees. Yummy!

PREP : 10 mins ● COOK : 15 mins ◙ SERV: 20

INGREDIENTS

Lemons	4
Chilly powder	4 tbs
Fenugreek powder	1 tsp
Asafetida	1/2 tsp
Salt	To taste
Garlic, peeled and cut into long slices	1/2 cup
Oil	1/2 cup
Vinegar	1 tbs

METHOD

- Wash the lemons and wipe them dry.

- Heat 1 tablespoon oil in a deep pan. Add the lemon whole and stir it in medium heat. When you see juice coming from the lemon remove the pan from heat. When it cools, cut each lemon into eight pieces.

- Heat the rest of the oil in the same pan, add garlic and stir. When the garlic turns light brown, turn to low heat. Add the chilly, fenugreek, asafetida, salt, and stir for 5 minutes. Add vinegar and heat well for 2 minutes. Combine the lemon pieces and salt, stirring continuously. Remove and store in a glass jar when cool.

MANGO PICKLE

Most people seem to prefer mango pickle over other pickles and there are innumerable variants of this king among pickles. So, shall we try a simple and easy to make version?

PREP : 10 mins   COOK : 15 mins   SERV: 8

INGREDIENTS

Green mango (1/2" pieces with skin)	1 cup
Chilly powder	3 tbs
Turmeric powder	1/2 tsp
Asafetida	1/4 tsp
Fenugreek powder	1/2 tsp
Salt	to taste
Mustard seeds	1 tsp
Fenugreek seeds	1 tsp
Water	1/4 cup
Oil	1/8 cup

METHOD

- Wash the lemons and wipe them dry.

- Heat 1 tablespoon oil in a deep pan. Add the lemon whole and stir it in medium heat. When you see juice coming from the lemon remove the pan from heat. When it cools, cut each lemon into eight pieces.

- Heat the rest of the oil in the same pan, add garlic and stir. When the garlic turns light brown, turn to low heat. Add the chilly, fenugreek, asafetida, salt, and stir for 5 minutes. Add vinegar and heat well for 2 minutes. Combine the lemon pieces and salt, stirring continuously. Remove and store in a glass jar when cool.

PULI INJI

Puli Inji is a sweet, spicy, and tangy tamarind and ginger pickle - hence the name. This pickle can be kept for a long time when refrigerated. Puli Inji is a great side dish for curd rice. It could also be used to prepare tamarind rice (puliodharai/puliogare).

🥄 PREP : 5 mins　🍲 COOK : 30 mins　📷 SERV: 20

INGREDIENTS

Tamarind	50 g
Ginger, chopped	3 tsp
Green chillies, chopped	1 tsp
Oil	2 tbs
Red chillies	2
Mustard seeds	2 tsp
Turmeric powder	1/2 tsp
Chilly powder	1 tsp
Asafetida	1/4 tsp
Jaggery	35 g
Fenugreek seeds	1/4 tsp
Curry leaves	5-8

METHOD

- Soak the tamarind in 1 cup of water. Drain to extract the tamarind juice and discard the pulp.

- Heat oil in a frying pan and splutter mustard seeds. Add whole red chillies and curry leaves. Stir and add chopped ginger and green chillies. Then add tamarind water, turmeric powder, chilly powder and asafetida and boil for about 30 minutes. When the gravy is thick, add the jaggery and boil for a few seconds more. Finally, add fenugreek.

DESSERTS

08

WHEAT PAYASAM

This easy to make traditional Kerala payasam is prepared with broken wheat, coconut milk, and jaggery. Broken wheat is a complex carbohydrate and an excellent source of fiber, especially good for diabetics.

PREP : 10 mins   COOK : 40 mins   SERV: 8

INGREDIENTS

Broken wheat	1/4 kg
Jaggery	1/4 kg
Water	1 liter
Coconut milk	3 cans
Cashewnuts chopped	2 tbs
Cumin seed powder	1/4 tsp
Cardamom powder	1/4 tsp
Dry ginger powder	1/4 tsp
Coconut bits	2 tbs
Ghee	1/8 cup

METHOD

- Wash the wheat. Fry the cashewnuts in 2 teaspoons ghee. Pour 2 cans of coconut milk into a bowl and add 1 can water. Boil 1 liter water in a large heavy pot. Then add the wheat and cook for 20 minutes. Stir the wheat constantly. When the wheat is half cooked, add jaggery and stir well. When the water dries up, add the ghee. Stir constantly for about 5 minutes.

- Combine coconut milk from the bowl and cook for 10 minutes, stirring continuously. When the mixture thickens, add cashewnuts, cumin powder, cardamom powder, dry ginger powder, coconut bits and remaining 1 can of coconut milk. Remove from heat and stir for 3 more minutes.

- Serve after 20 minutes.

PARIPPU (MOONG DAL) PAYASAM

A delicious payasam made for special occasions like Onam.

PREP : 6 mins ♦ COOK : 50 mins ▨ SERV: 10

INGREDIENTS

Moong dal	1-1/2 cups
Boiled water	2 cups
Jaggery	2 cups
Ghee	1 tbs
Coconut bits	3/4 cup
Coconut milk	3 cans
Chukku (dry ginger powder)	1 tsp
Water	3 Cups

METHOD

• Boil water in a pot and dissolve jaggery. Drain it to remove impurities. Wash the dal and drain the water. Fry the coconut bits in 2 teaspoon ghee until they turn brown and remove from flame. Mix 2 cans of coconut milk with 1 can of water in a bowl and set aside.

• Fry the dal in a deep-frying pan until the dal is roasted. Pour 2 cups of boiled water and cook in medium heat for 30 minutes, stirring it well. When the dal is half cooked, add jaggery and ghee. Stir well for about 20 minutes. Add the coconut milk from the bowl, continuously stirring the mixture until it thickens a bit. Add the coconut bits, dry ginger powder, and the last can of coconut milk. Remove from heat and keep stirring for another minute. Keep aside for 20 minutes before serving.

SEMIYA PAYASAM

This is a very easy to make dessert. Considered in some circles to be "too simple" a dish, semiya payasam, nevertheless, is a clear favorite with children (including my own) who yearn for this treat whenever possible!

PREP : 10 mins COOK : 35 mins SERV: 5

INGREDIENTS

Semiya	1/2 kg
Milk	3 liters
Water	1-1/2 liters
Sugar	1 kg
Cashewnuts (split into half)	1/2 cup
Raisins	1 tbs
Cardamoms	6
Ghee	1/4 cup

METHOD

- Heat a pan, pour 2 teaspoons ghee and add cashewnuts and raisins. Stir until the cashewnuts are roasted and then remove. Combine with crushed cardamoms.

- In the same pan, add 3 teaspoons of ghee. Add semiya and fry until it turns brown and then transfer it to a plate. In another pan, mix water and 2 liters of milk together. Boil for about 20 minutes, stirring constantly. Combine the semiya into this boiling milk. Continue to boil until the semiya is cooked. Add sugar. When the milk thickens add the rest of the milk little by little while constantly stirring it. Add the roasted cashewnuts, raisins, crushed cardamoms and the remaining ghee, and stir for a couple of minutes. Keep aside for about 20 minutes and then serve.

UTENSIL GLOSSARY

A list of indigenous vessels from India that are used in some of the recipes in this book.

Appa Chatty	A special curved pan (available in Kerala stores), which gives appam a lacy border.
Appakara	A special pan for deep frying unniappam/neyyappam. Appakaras come in various sizes – accommodating 4, 5, or 7 unniappams.
Dhokla Steamer	A steamer with flat plates to steam dhokla – a Gujarati dish. Could be used for making Vattappam.
Idli Cooker	A vessel with idli mold plates and holder for steaming idlis.
Idli Spoon	Any suitable spoon to take the idlis out from the idli thattu.
Idli Steamer	Idli cooker.
Idli Thattu	Idli cooker plates.
Manchatti	A metal made large flat wok or griddle used to make flatbreads. Used for making chapatti, dosa or to shallow fry.
Mini Idli Cooker	An idli cooker with special plates for making bite sized mini idlis.
Seva Nazhi with Chillu	A press with different circular mold plates (chillu) used for making sevai, pakkavada, murukku, etc.
Tawa	Dosa pan.
Uruli	A wide, shallow, and thick vessel used on special occasions to cook large quantities of food.

GLOSSARY

All purpose flour	A plain flour without any leavening agent.
Amla	Gooseberry
Asafetida	Hing. A brownish gum resin with strong taste and odor.
Baking powder	A powder used in baking for leavening
Basmati rice	A long grained fragrant Indian rice with a delicate flavor.
Besan	Chickpea flour or Bengal gram flour
Biryani	A rice dish where rice and curry (veg or meat) are cooked separately and then layered resulting in contrasting flavors.
Black pepper	Kali Mirch. Pepper that is ground from whole peppercorns with husks on.
Bread crumbs	Crumb of bread used for thickening or coating
Broken wheat	Wheat rava or cracked wheat.
Brown sugar	unrefined or partly refined sugar, jaggery
Cardamom	An aromatic seed used for seasoning, elaichi
Cashewnut	A kidney shaped nut
Cassava	A root rich in starch. Also known as tapioca.
Celery	An aromatic herb used for seasoning
Chana dal	Split chickpeas
Chicken masala powder	A masala used for flavoring chicken
Chickpea flour (besan)	Bengal gram flour
Chickpeas	Chana
Chukku	Dry ginger
Cinnamon	Aromatic bark used as spice
Clove	Aromatic flower bud used as a spice
Coconut bits	coconut cut into small pieces
Coconut milk	White liquid obtained by compressing coconut

Coconut water	Clear fluid from fresh coconut
Coriander leaves	Parsley-like herb used for seasoning
Coriander seeds	Dhania
Corn flour	starch prepared from corn, used as a thickener
Cream	The part of milk containing butter fat
Cucumber	A cylindrical green vegetable
Cumin seeds	Aromatic seed, jeera
Curd	A diary product from the fermentation of milk.
Dal	Lentil
Dhana Jeera	Coriander and cumin mixture
Drumstick	A vegetable
Eggplant	Egg shaped vegetable with a purple skin
Fennel seeds	Anise seed, saunf
Fenugreek	Aromatic seed used for seasoning, kasoori methi
Gambooge (kudampuli)	Kudampuli is a green fruit that turns yellow when ripe. Kudampuli gets the black color after it is processed and will stay fresh for years.
Garam masala	A blend of cumin, pepper, cloves and cardamom
Garlic	A pungent aromatic bulb used for seasoning
Garlic paste	A paste made from garlic
Ghee	Clarified butter
Ginger	A pungent rhizome used as seasoning, Adrak.
Ginger paste	A paste made from ginger
Ginger-garlic paste	Ginger and garlic mix
Green mango	Raw mango
Green pepper	A sweet pepper that becomes red when ripe
Green plantains	Raw banana
Idli batter	Batter that could be used for making idli, dosa, uthappam, etc
Idli rice	Parboiled rice

Jaggery or brown sugar	Unrefined brown sugar
Khus khus	Poppy seeds
King Fish	A large and expensive fish with an oily flesh
Liquid mustard	A pungent paste prepared from ground mustard seeds
Long beans	Yard long beans
Long grain white rice	A rice with a grain that is 3-4 times longer than its width and when cooked is soft, fluffy and with separate grains.
Margarine	A vegetable oil spread used as a substitute for butter
Mint leaves	Aromatic leaves used fresh as a seasoning
Moong	Green gram. Whole green lentils.
Moong dal	Split green gram
Mustard seeds	Small round black seeds used as a condiment.
Mutton	Goat meat.
Oil	Cooking oil.
Okra	Lady's fingers
Palaharam	A light snack or tiffin.
Pappad	A thin crisp Indian snack that could be served as an appetizer or as a side dish.
Patna Rice	A variety of long grain rice.
Peanuts	Groundnuts
Plantain	Raw banana
Plantain leaf	Banana leaf. A traditional Kerala meal such as Onam Sadhya is served on a plantain leaf.
Prawns	Chemmeen.
Raisins	Dried grapes.
Rava	Semolina. Sooji
Romaine Lettuce	A variety of lettuce with big sturdy leaves that are tolerant to heat.
Saffron	Spice derived from the stigma of the saffron flower. It is the most expensive spice in the world since the stigmas have to be handpicked and each flower has only a few of them.

Sago	Sabudana/javvarisi. Sago is a produce prepared from tapioca root.
Toor dal	Red gram dal or urad dal
Sambar powder	Spice mix for sambar. Roasted lentils, coriander seeds, red chillies, fenugreek, and curry leaves ground into a coarse powder to be used when preparing sambar.
Sardines	A common type of fish. Mathi in Malayalam.
Sesame seeds	Ellu. A condiment with a rich nutty flavor.
Shrimp	A species of fish similar in appearance to prawn.
Small red onions	Sambar onions.
Sooji	See Rava.
String beans	Green beans.
Tamarind	Puli. A sweet and sour fruit used for flavoring.
Tamarind puree	Tamarind extract.
Tandoori color	Red or yellow food coloring.
Tandoori masala	Spice mix for tandoori cooking.
Tuna	A fish with pink or red flesh.
Turmeric powder	A spice used as a coloring agent.
Unakkalari rice	A hand pounded, short grain, brown rice. Unakkalari is considered to be an aristocratic rice variety and lends to the payasam a rich flavor and a creamy texture.
Urad dal	Split black lentils.
Vinegar	Vinegar is used to tenderize meat by marinating. It is also used to enhance shelf life of pickles.
White flour	Refined flour
Whole black pepper	A pungent spice.
Yam	An edible tuber.
Yeast	A leavening agent used to raise dough
Yellow split peas	Matar dal

Kindly send errors, corrections, and suggestions to cpathiyal@gmail.com. Thank you.

Printed in Great Britain
by Amazon

45946892R00059